SO-AIS-635

DOG BREEDS

West Highland White Terriers

by Sara Green

Consultant:
Michael Leuthner, D.V.M.
PetCare Clinic, Madison, Wisc.

MAR 2 8 2011

BELLWETHER MEDIA • MINNEAPOLIS, MN

Note to Librarians, Teachers, and Parents:

Blastoff! Readers are carefully developed by literacy experts and combine standards-based content with developmentally appropriate text.

Level 1 provides the most support through repetition of high-frequency words, light text, predictable sentence patterns, and strong visual support.

Level 2 offers early readers a bit more challenge through varied simple sentences, increased text load, and less repetition of high-frequency words.

Level 3 advances early-fluent readers toward fluency through increased text and concept load, less reliance on visuals, longer sentences, and more literary language.

Level 4 builds reading stamina by providing more text per page, increased use of punctuation, greater variation in sentence patterns, and increasingly challenging vocabulary.

Level 5 encourages children to move from "learning to read" to "reading to learn" by providing even more text, varied writing styles, and less familiar topics.

Whichever book is right for your reader, Blastoff! Readers are the perfect books to build confidence and encourage a love of reading that will last a lifetime!

This edition first published in 2010 by Bellwether Media, Inc.

No part of this publication may be reproduced in whole or in part without written permission of the publisher. For information regarding permission, write to Bellwether Media, Inc., Attention: Permissions Department, 5357 Penn Avenue South, Minneapolis, MN 55419.

Library of Congress Cataloging-in-Publication Data
Green, Sara, 1964–
West Highland white terriers / by Sara Green.
    p. cm. — (Blastoff! readers dog breeds)
Includes bibliographical references and index.
    Summary: "Simple text and full-color photography introduce beginning readers to the characteristics of the dog breed West Highland White Terriers. Developed by literacy experts for students in kindergarten through third grade"—Provided by publisher.
    ISBN 978-1-60014-300-7 (hardcover : alk. paper)
    1. West Highland white terrier—Juvenile literature. I. Title.
SF429.W4G74 2010
636.755—dc22
                              2009037214

Text copyright © 2010 by Bellwether Media, Inc. BLASTOFF! READERS and associated logos are trademarks and/or registered trademarks of Bellwether Media, Inc.

Printed in the United States of America, North Mankato, MN.
010110   1149

Contents

What Are West Highland
White Terriers?   4

History of West Highland
White Terriers   8

West Highland White
Terriers Today   14

Glossary   22

To Learn More   23

Index   24

What Are West Highland White Terriers?

West Highland White Terriers are small, friendly dogs with shiny, white **coats**. They are also called Westies. They belong to the **Terrier Group** of dogs. Adult Westies weigh 15 to 22 pounds (7 to 10 kilograms). They are 10 to 11 inches (25 to 28 centimeters) tall at the shoulder.

Westies have **double coats**. They have an undercoat and an outer coat. The hair of the undercoat is short and soft. It helps Westies stay warm in cold temperatures. The hair of the outer coat is long and straight. It keeps the undercoat and skin clean and dry.

! **fun fact**

The Westie's outer coat is rough and wiry. The wiry hair stands up around the Westie's face. This makes its face look round.

History of West Highland White Terriers

The **ancestor** of the Westie is the Cairn Terrier. This **breed** is from Scotland. Cairn Terriers have dark coats. In the 19th century, people used Cairn Terriers to hunt small animals that lived underground.

Some Cairn Terrier **litters** included puppies with white coats. Many people thought terriers with white coats were weak. They did not think white terriers could hunt.

! fun fact

The word *terrier* comes from a Latin word that means *earth*.

A Scottish man named Edward Donald Malcolm had a different idea. He thought dogs with white coats would make good hunting dogs. It would be easier for hunters to recognize their white dogs in the fields and woods.

Malcolm decided to breed white terriers. He called them Poltalloch Terriers.

Other people started breeding white terriers. Breeders could not agree on one name for the white terriers. They were called different names such as Roseneath Terriers and White Scottish Terriers.

The Scottish Kennel Club decided that white terriers should have one name. In 1904, they chose to call the breed the West Highland White Terrier.

West Highland White Terriers Today

! fun fact

The nails of Westies and other terriers grow faster than those of other breeds. Long nails help Westies dig holes in the ground very quickly.

Westies are not used for hunting anymore. Today, they are popular family pets. Westies still have behaviors that are similar to the hunting behaviors of their ancestors. They chase animals such as squirrels and chipmunks. They dig holes in the ground. Some Westies dig to look for small animals. Most Westies dig just for fun!

Westies are smart **working dogs**. They can learn skills that help people. Some Westies work as hearing dogs for people who are deaf.

These Westies are trained to touch deaf people with their paws or noses when sounds occur at home. The Westies tell deaf people when people knock on their doors, babies cry, or smoke alarms beep.

Some Westies participate in **flyball**. Flyball is a relay race where dog teams race each other on a course. The course has four hurdles.

Each dog on the team must jump over the hurdles, retrieve a ball, and return back over the hurdles to cross the finish line. The team with the fastest time and fewest errors wins!

Westies have a lot of energy. They are always on the lookout for a playmate. If they cannot find one, Westies will make their own fun. They enjoy running in the yard, chasing balls, and digging for buried treasure. Life with a Westie is never boring!

Glossary

ancestor—a family member who lived long ago

breed—a type of dog

coat—the hair or fur of an animal

double coat—a coat of an animal with an over coat and an undercoat

flyball—a relay race for dogs

litter—a group of young born from one mother at the same time

Terrier Group—a group of dogs bred to hunt small animals that live underground

working dogs—a breed of dog that does jobs to help people

To Learn More

AT THE LIBRARY

American Kennel Club. *The Complete Dog Book for Kids*. New York, N.Y.: Howell Books, 1996.

Anjou, Colette. *Westie The Dog*. Washington, D.C.: E & E Publishing, 2005.

Hubbard, Coleen. *The Westie Winter*. Ferndale, Wash.: Apple, 1999.

ON THE WEB

Learning more about West Highland White Terriers is as easy as 1, 2, 3.

1. Go to www.factsurfer.com.

2. Enter "West Highland White Terriers" into the search box.

3. Click the "Surf" button and you will see a list of related Web sites.

With factsurfer.com, finding more information is just a click away.

Index

1904, 13
ancestor, 8, 15
breed, 8, 13, 14
Cairn Terrier, 8, 9
coats, 5, 6, 7, 8, 9, 10
digging, 14, 15, 21
double coat, 6
flyball, 18, 19
hearing dogs, 16, 17
height, 5
hunting, 8, 9, 10, 15
hurdles, 18, 19
litters, 9
Malcolm, Edward
   Donald, 10, 11
outer coat, 6, 7
Poltalloch Terriers, 11
Roseneath Terriers, 12

Scotland, 8
Scottish Kennel Club, 13
Terrier Group, 5
undercoat, 6
White Scottish Terriers,
   12
working dogs, 16

The images in this book are reproduced through the courtesy of: Eric Isselee, front cover; Nicky Dronoff-Guthrie, pp. 4-5; Faith A. Uriel/Kimballstock, pp. 5, 10, 11; Juniors Bildarchiv, pp. 6, 8, 9; Juan Martinez, pp. 6-7, 14-15, 16; Martin Ruegner, p. 12; Mark Raycraft, p. 13; Jo Sax, p. 15; Gerard Brown, p. 17; Willie Moore, pp. 18, 19; F. Lukasseck, pp. 20-21; ARCO/P. Wegner, p. 21.